Most Lawyers Are Liars

The Truth about LLC's - C Corporations – S Corporations and 501 3 C's

Written by

The Money Guy and The Tax Guy

1

You want to go into business – well, you're going to need to be a company in some way shape or form. Here are the main tools that are sold to people by lawyers that are overpriced due to lack of understanding. This will help you get a better understanding and might save you a lot of money up front.

LLC vs. S Corporation: An Overview

Choosing the right business structure is crucial to the success of your business.

An LLC is a limited liability company, which is a type of legal entity that can be used when forming a business. An LLC offers a more formal business structure than a sole proprietorship or partnership. It also offers protection to the owner from personal liability for any of the debts that a business incurs. In other words, the personal assets of the owner cannot be used for legal claims against the business. LLCs are common because they provide the liability that is like a corporation, but they are easier to establish.

While LLCs and S corporations two terms are often discussed side-by-side, they refer to various aspects of a business. An LLC is a type of business entity, while an S corporation is a tax classification. It lets the Internal Revenue Service (IRS) know that your business should be taxed as a partnership. To become an S-corporation, your business first must register as a C corporation or an LLC. A business must meet specific guidelines by the Internal Revenue Service (IRS) to qualify as an S corporation.

An S corporation provides limited liability protection but also offers corporations with one hundred shareholders or fewer to be taxed as a partnership. An S corporation is also known as an S subchapter. In some instances, a business may be both an LLC and an S-corporation. (You can form an LLC and choose to be taxed as an S corporation, but your business can also operate under the default taxation system for LLCs.)

The business structure that you choose can significantly impact some critical issues in your business life. These issues include exposure to liability and at what rate and manner you and your business are taxed. It can also impact your financing and your ability to grow the business, the number of shareholders the business has, and the general way the business is operated.

Both LLCs and S corporations surged to the forefront around the time of the Small Business Job Protection Act of 1996, which contained several changes to basic corporate tax law, such as enabling S corporations to hold any percentage of stock in C corporations. C corporations, however, are not allowed to own stock in S corporations.

Key Takeaways

- An LLC is a limited liability company, which is a type of legal entity that can be used when forming a business.

- An LLC offers a more formal business structure than a sole proprietorship or partnership.

- While LLCs and S corporations two terms are often discussed side-by-side, they refer to various aspects of a business.

- An LLC is a type of business entity, while an S corporation is a tax classification.

- An S corporation election lets the Internal Revenue Service (IRS) know that your business should be taxed as a partnership.

- To become an S-corporation, your business first must register as a C corporation or an LLC and meet specific guidelines by the Internal Revenue Service (IRS) to qualify.

Limited Liability Company (LLC)

Limited liability companies (LLCs) are popular due to their basic benefits of liability protection and are typically used by a sole proprietor (single owner) or a company with two or more owners (partnership). LLCs protect the owners' personal assets from losses, company debts, or court rulings against the company. LLCs may also provide some tax benefits since they are taxed differently than a traditional corporation—or a C Corporation.

An LLC can be used for a company of any size, such as a doctor's or dentist's office, or as a legal entity that owns commercial property. Also, an LLC can be established by family members who conduct business in states that allow LLCs. Before establishing an LLC, entrepreneurs should consider the various characteristics that are associated with forming an LLC, which include the following.

Ownership of an LLC

An LLC is allowed to have an unlimited number of owners, commonly referred to as "members." These owners may be U.S. citizens, non-U.S. citizens, and non-U.S. residents. Also, LLCs may be owned by any other type of corporate entity, and an LLC faces less regulation regarding the formation of subsidiaries.

LLC Business Operations

For LLCs, business operations are much simpler than other corporate structures, and the requirements are minimal. While LLCs are urged to follow the same guidelines as S corporations, they are not legally required to do so. Some of these guidelines include adopting bylaws and conducting annual meetings.

For example, instead of the detailed requirements for corporate bylaws for S corporations, LLCs merely adopt an LLC operating agreement, the terms of which can be extremely flexible, allowing the owners to set up the business to operate in whatever fashion they most prefer. LLCs are not required to keep and maintain records of company meetings and decisions in the way that S corporations are required to do.

Management Structure of an LLC

The owners or members of an LLC are free to choose whether the owners or designated managers run the business. If the LLC elects to have the owners occupy the company management positions, then the business would operate similarly to a partnership.

LLC Taxation and Fees

Limited liability companies are taxed differently from other corporations. An LLC allows pass-through taxation, which is when the business income or losses pass through the business and are instead recorded on the owner's personal tax return. As a result, the profits are taxed at the owner's personal tax rate. A single-member LLC is typically taxed as a sole proprietorship. Any profits, losses, or deductions that are business expenses that reduce taxable income are all reported on the owner's personal tax return. An LLC with multiple owners would be taxed as a partnership, meaning each owner would report profit and losses on their personal tax return.

LLCs avoid the double taxation to which C corporations must pay because they pass all company income through to the tax returns of the individual owners. A C corporation (or C-Corp) is a legal structure for a corporation in which the owners, or shareholders, are taxed separately from the entity. C corporations, the most prevalent of corporations, are also subject to corporate income taxation. The taxing of profits from the business is at both corporate and personal levels, creating a double taxation situation.

The fees for establishing an LLC can vary by state but expect to pay $500, which might include the following:

• Articles of incorporation fee, which might cost $100

• Annual reporting fees, which can cost a few hundred dollars per year

• Attorney fees if you have a lawyer draw up the legal documents

• Tax and accounting fees if you use an accounting firm to prepare financials and file taxes

How to Form an LLC

Below are several of the steps involved in forming an LLC. However, please check with your local state since they may have additional forms and requirements.

1. Choose a name. The company name should follow the state guidelines in which the LLC will be formed. Also, the chosen name cannot already be an existing business name that is recorded and established.

2. Assign a registered agent. Your LLC may be required to have a registered agent, which is a person or company that oversees any legal papers on behalf of the LLC if there is a lawsuit. Your local office of the Secretary of State should have a listing of local companies that can function as a registered agent.

3. File articles of organization with your local office for Secretary of State. The articles of organization might also be called a certificate of formation or certificate of organization. Articles of organization are legal forms that outline basic information about the company, and each state

may have specific requirements. However, most states usually require the following: the name and address of the LLC, a description of the general purpose of the LLC, a list of the owners, and the name and address of the registered agent.

4. Create an operating agreement. An operating agreement is an internal document that stipulates how the LLC will be run and how it will be managed. The operating agreement should include procedures for how members will be managed if there are more than one and how profits and losses will be divided between the members. The operating agreement should also outline the procedures for adding new members and when members leave. If an operating agreement is not in place and a member leaves, a state may require the LLC to be dissolved. However, the operating agreement does not need to be filed with your state's office. Instead, it should be kept within your business records and updated, as necessary.

5. Apply for a federal ID number, if necessary. If you have more than one owner, you'll need to establish an employer identification number (EIN), which is a federal ID number that identifies the company. If you are a sole proprietor, you do not necessarily need an EIN number unless you want it taxed as a corporation instead of a sole proprietorship.

6. File business licenses, permits, and establish a bank account. It is important to check with your local state, county, and town offices to determine if there are business licenses and permits that need to be filed. Depending on the type of business that you will be operating, your state may require a permit or license to be in place before you can begin operating your business. Also, if the LLC will be selling goods that are subject to a local sales tax, you will need to file with your local tax office so that you can collect the sales taxes and remit them to the state.

7. It is important to note that the above list is not comprehensive since each state may have additional requirements. Once established, many states require LLCs to file an annual report, which the state may charge a fee. These fees can sometimes run in the hundreds of dollars per year.

LLC Pros and Cons

There are distinct advantages and disadvantages to establishing and operating a limited liability company.

LLC Pros

As stated earlier, an LLC gives the owner or owners limited liability, which means that each owner is not personally liable for any company related lawsuits or any debts that belong to the company. In other words, creditors cannot take or collect money from your personal assets to satisfy the debts of the business. Creditors are only able to take assets from the company.

LLCs are simpler to establish and operate when compared to a corporation. Corporations typically must have appointed directors, officers, and board meetings.

LLC's also have tax benefits since the company's income, or losses are reported on the owner's personal tax return. This prevents the profit generated from the business from being taxed at the business level and taxed again at the personal level when the owner takes a salary from the company. Instead, the profit from the business passes through the business entity and is only reported once for tax purposes on the owner's personal tax return.

Another benefit of LLCs is that they are extremely flexible when it comes to their structure. There are no limits to the number of owners, called members, and LLCs can operate with only one owner, like a sole proprietorship. LLCs also allow the owner to designate a manager to run the business, which could be one of the designated members, a non-member, or some combination of both.

LLC Cons

One of the disadvantages of an LLC is when ownership needs an injection of cash or money. If the LLC had gotten turned down for a bank loan, it could be difficult for the owner to attract money from outside investors. A corporation might be able to raise cash from venture capitalist firms, which provide money to businesses in exchange for a share of the profits. Venture capitalists usually only fund corporations and not privately owned LLCs.

An LLC can be more costly to form and operate when compared to a sole proprietorship or a partnership. As stated earlier, there can be filing fees for an EIN number and annual fees for filing the annual report.

Pros
• Personal liability protection

• No double taxation

• Easier to establish and operate than a corporation

• Flexible structure
Cons
• More costly to establish than a sole proprietorship or partnership

• Must file an annual report, and the fee can cost hundreds of dollars

• Cannot attract outside investment other than banks
The choice of business entity is going to be guided by the nature of the business and how the owner envisions the business unfolding and growing in the future.

S Corporations

An S corporation's structure also protects business owners' personal assets from any corporate liability and passes through income, usually in the form of dividends, to avoid double corporate and personal taxation.5 Below are some of the characteristics of s corporations.

Ownership of an S Corporation

The IRS is more restrictive regarding ownership for S corporations. These businesses are not allowed to have more than one hundred principal shareholders or owners. S corporations cannot be owned by individuals who are not U.S. citizens or permanent residents. Further, the S corporation cannot be owned by any other corporate entity. This limitation includes ownership by other S corporations, C corporations, LLCs, business partnerships, or sole proprietorships.

S Corporation Business Operations

There are significant legal differences in terms of formal operational requirements, with S corporations being much more rigidly structured. The numerous internal formalities required for S corporations include strict regulations on adopting corporate bylaws, conducting initial and annual shareholders meetings, keeping, and retaining company meeting minutes, and extensive regulations related to issuing stock shares.

Further, an S Corporation may use either accrual or cash basis accounting practices.

Management Structure of S Corporations

In contrast, S corporations are required to have a board of directors and corporate officers. The board of directors oversees the management and oversees major corporate decisions, while the corporate officers, such as the chief executive officer (CEO) and chief financial officer (CFO), manage the company's business operations on a day-to-day basis.

Other differences include the fact that an S corporation's existence, once established, is usually perpetual, while this is not typically the case with an LLC, where events such as the departure of a member/owner may result in the dissolution of the LLC.

LLCs and S corporations are business structures that impact a company's exposure to liability and how the business and business owner(s) are taxed.

S Corporation Taxation and Fees

S corporations can elect to pass corporate income, losses, deductions, and credits through to their shareholders for federal tax purposes. The shareholders of the S corporation would report the flow-through of income and losses on their personal tax returns. As a result, the assessed tax would be calculated based on their individual income tax rates. This pass-through feature helps S corporations to avoid double taxation, meaning the company's income is taxed at the corporate level and again when dividend income paid to shareholders is taxed on their personal income tax returns.

S Corporations must use Form 1120S to file their taxes. Form 1120S is a tax document that is used to report the income, losses, and dividends of S corporation shareholders

The fees to establish an S corporation can vary significantly, depending on the complexity of the corporation and state in which it is established, but some of the fees can include:
• Fees for the articles of incorporation, which might be $100 to $250, depending on the state

• Lawyer fees to process the legal documents can range from a few hundred dollars to a few thousand dollars if the S corporation structure is more complex

• Annual reporting fees within the state might be required and can cost $500 to $800 per year

• Accounting costs for financial reporting and tax services should be considered

• Insurance costs can vary depending on the type of business

How to Form an S Corporation

1. Choose a name. The company name should be chosen that is not already in use within the jurisdiction of the S corporation. Typically, the local state or town offices will have a listing of the existing corporations in the area so that you can avoid choosing a name that already exists.

2. Establish and name the board of directors. A board of directors is an elected group of individuals that function as a governing body representing the shareholders. The board is required to meet at regular intervals and keep minutes for the meetings. The board is also required to establish policies for the management team. Every S corporation must have a board of directors. Issuance of stock for the S Corporation can be in the form of common or preferred stock.

3. File articles of organization with both the IRS and the local office for Secretary of State. In addition to the articles of organization, it might be required to file a document separately stating the purpose of the business. Although the guidelines can vary by state, many states require the following information: Names and contact information of the management team and the board of directors

4. Name of the S corporation

5. Number of shares issued

6. How shares are allocated

7. Registered agent name

8. File the corporate bylaws. A document outlining the corporate bylaws is usually required to be filed with the local Secretary of State office. It typically outlines the procedures for the following: Electing and removing directors:

9. How shares of stock will be sold

10. Holding meetings

11. Voting rights

12. How the death of a director or officer will be managed

13. File Form 2553 with the IRS. Once a certificate of incorporation has been received from your local Secretary of State office showing that the S corporation has been organized, you must file form 2553 with the IRS. The form is called the Election by a Small Business Corporation, which makes the company official with the Internal Revenue Service.

14. File with a registered agent. Many states require that a registered agent be to be assigned for the S corporation. The agent should receive all legal documents and correspondence between state and federal agencies.

S Corporations Pros and Cons

There are distinct advantages and disadvantages to establishing and operating an S corporation. Some of the advantages include:

Pros

An S corporation usually does not pay federal taxes at the corporate level. As a result, an S corporation can help the owner save money on corporate taxes. The S corporation allows the owner to report the taxes on their personal tax return, like an LLC or sole proprietorship.

An established S corporation can help boost credibility with suppliers, investors, and customers since it shows a commitment to the company and to the shareholders. S corporations allow the owner to benefit from personal liability protection, which prevents personal assets from being taken by creditors to satisfy a business debt. Also, employees of an S Corp are also members, which means they are eligible to receive cash payments via dividends from the company's profits. Dividends can be a great incentive for employees to work there and help the owner attract talented workers.

There are also some disadvantages to establishing and operating an S Corporation.

Cons

Although most states allow the income generated from an S corporation to be taxed on the owner's personal tax returns, some states do not. In other words, some states choose to tax an S corporation as if it was a corporation. It is important to check with your local Secretary of State office to determine how S corporations are taxed in your state.

S corporations can incur a number of fees, including those for filing an annual report, hiring a registered agent, which handles legal matters for the business, and other fees for the Articles of Incorporation filed with the local Secretary of State office.

S corporations can be more cumbersome to establish and operate than an LLC since they require a board of directors and corporate officers. Also, filing guidelines and regulations are more rigid for S corporation vs. LLCs, including for the annual shareholder meetings, issuance of stock shares, and keeping meeting minutes.

Pros

• Provides personal liability protection

- Does not pay taxes at the corporate level, allowing pass-through to a personal tax return

- Can boost credibility with suppliers, creditors, and investors

- Pays dividends to employees

Cons

- Some states may tax S corporations as corporations, not at the personal level.

- S corporations can incur more fees than an LLC.

- S corporations have more regulations and guidelines that must be followed.

- Owner has less control.

Special Considerations

A business owner who wants to have the maximum amount of personal asset protection plans on seeking substantial investment from outsiders or envisions eventually becoming a publicly traded company and selling common stock will likely be best served by forming a C corporation and then making the S corporation tax election.

It is important to understand that the S corporation designation is merely a tax choice made to have your business taxed according to Subchapter S of Chapter 1 of the Internal Revenue Service Code. An S corporation might begin as some other business entity, such as a sole proprietorship or an LLC. The business then elects to become an S corporation for tax purposes.

LLC vs. S Corp FAQs

What Is the Difference Between an LLC and an S Corp?

A limited liability company is easier to establish and has fewer regulatory requirements than other corporations. LLCs allow for personal liability protection, which means creditors cannot go after the owner's personal assets. An LLC allows pass-through taxation, meaning business income or losses are recorded and taxed on the owner's personal tax return. LLCs are beneficial for sole proprietorships and partnerships. An LLC with multiple owners would be taxed as a partnership, meaning each owner would report profit and losses on their personal tax return.

An S corporation's structure also protects business owners' personal assets from any corporate liability and passes through income, usually in the form of dividends, to avoid double corporate and personal taxation. S corporations help companies establish credibility as a corporation since they have more oversight. S corps must have a board of directors who oversee the management of the company. However, S corps can have100 shareholders and pay them dividends or cash payments from the company's profits.

Which Is Better, an LLC or S Corp?

An LLC is better for a single-owner and better for a partnership. An LLC is more appropriate for business owners whose primary concern is business management flexibility. This owner wants to avoid all, but a minimum of corporate paperwork does not project a need for extensive outside investment and does not plan to take her company public and selling the stock.

In general, the smaller, simpler, and more personally managed the business is, the more appropriate the LLC structure would be for the owner. If your business is larger and more complex, an S corporation structure would be more appropriate.

Who Pays More Taxes, an LLC, or S Corp?

It depends on how the business is established for tax purposes and how much profit is going to be generated. Both an LLC and S Corp can be taxed at the personal income tax level. LLCs are often taxed using personal rates, but some LLC owners choose to be taxed as a separate entity with its own federal ID number. S corporation owners must be paid a salary in which they pay Social Security and Medicare taxes. However, dividend income or some of the remaining profits (after the owner's salary has been paid) can be passed through to the owner, but not as an employee, meaning they will not pay Social Security and Medicare taxes on those funds.

Why Would You Choose an S Corporation?

An S corporation provides limited liability protection so that personal assets cannot be taken to satisfy business debts by creditors. S corporations also can help the owner save money on corporate taxes since it allows the owner to report the income that is passed through the business to the owner to be taxed at the personal income tax rate. If there will be multiple people involved in running the company, an S Corp would be better than an LLC since there would be oversight via the board of directors. Also, members can be employees, and an S Corp allows the members to receive cash dividends from company profits, which can be a great employee benefit.

Should I Make My LLC an S Corp?

If you are a sole proprietor, it might be best to establish an LLC since your business assets are separated from your personal assets. You can always change the structure later or create a new company that is an S corporation. An S corporation would be better for more complex companies with many people involved since there needs to be a board of directors, a maximum of one hundred shareholders, and more regulatory requirements.

The Bottom Line

LLCs are easier and less expensive to set up and simpler to maintain and remain compliant with the applicable business laws since there are less stringent operational regulations and reporting requirements. Nonetheless, the S corporation format is preferable if the business is seeking substantial outside financing or if it will eventually issue common stock.

It is, of course, possible to change the structure of a business if the nature of the business changes to require it but doing so often might involve incurring a tax penalty of one kind or another. Therefore, it is best if the business owner can determine the most appropriate business entity choice when first establishing the business.

In addition to the basic legal requirements for various types of business entities that are generally codified at the federal level, there are variations between state laws regarding incorporation. Therefore, it is considered a clever idea to consult with a corporate lawyer or accountant to make an informed decision regarding what type of business entity is best suited for your specific business.

What Is an S Corporation (S Subchapter)?

An S corporation, also known as an S subchapter, refers to a type of corporation that meets specific Internal Revenue Code requirements. If it does, it may pass income (along with other credits, deductions, and losses) directly to shareholders, without having to pay federal corporate taxes. Usually associated with small businesses (one hundred or fewer shareholders), S Corp status effectively gives a business the regular benefits of incorporation while enjoying the tax-exempt privileges of a partnership.

Key Takeaways
• An S corporation, also known as an S subchapter, refers to a type of legal business entity.

• Requirements give a corporation with one hundred shareholders or less the benefit of incorporation while being taxed as a partnership.

• Corporate taxes filed under Subchapter S may pass business income, losses, deductions, and credits to shareholders.

• Shareholders report income and losses on individual tax returns and pay taxes at ordinary tax rates.

• S corporation shareholders must be individuals, specific trusts and estates, or certain tax-exempt organizations.

Understanding S Corporations (S Subchapters)

To obtain an S corporation status, a business must meet certain IRS requirements. These qualifications include1

- being incorporated domestically (within the U.S.)

- having only one class of stock

- not having more than one hundred shareholders

- have shareholders who meet certain eligibility requirements

Specifically, S corporation shareholders must be individuals, specific trusts and estates, or certain tax-exempt organizations (501(c)(3). Partnerships, corporations, and nonresident aliens cannot qualify as eligible shareholders.

S corporations get their name from Subchapter S of the Internal Revenue Code, under which they have elected to be taxed. The key characteristic of a corporation filed under Subchapter S: It may pass business income, losses, deductions, and credits directly to shareholders, without paying any federal corporate tax—something known as a "pass-through" entity. It is liable on the corporate level for taxes on specific built-in gains and passive income, however.

S Corp shareholders report income, gains, and losses from the corporation on their individual tax returns and pay taxes at their ordinary income tax rates. Since the money comes to them free of corporate tax, or they avoid double taxation on any income or earnings.

Aside from its tax status, an S Corp is similar to any other corporation, or C corporation as they're officially known. It is a for-profit company, incorporated under and governed by the same state corporation laws. It offers similar liability protection, ownership, and management advantages as a C corporation. It must also observe internal practices and formalities: have a board of directors, write corporate bylaws, conduct shareholders' meetings, and keep minutes of significant company meetings.

IRS Form 2553

To create an S corporation, a business must first be incorporated.

It then must file Form 2553 with the IRS. Known officially as "Election by a Small Business Corporation," the form states that IRS will accept the S Corp status only if the business meets all the qualifications for the status, "all shareholders have signed the consent statement, an officer has signed below, and the exact name and address of the corporation (entity) and other required form information have been provided." Advantages and Disadvantages of S Corporations

Advantages of Filing Under Subchapter S

The big advantage of registering as an S corporation is the tax benefit: not having to pay federal taxes at the entity level.2 Saving money on corporate taxes is beneficial, especially when a business is in its early years.

S Corp status can lower the personal income tax tab for the business owners as well. By characterizing

14

money, they receive from the business as salary or dividends, S corporation owners often lower their liability for self-employment tax. The S Corp status generates deductions for business expenses and wages paid their employees too.

S Corp shareholders can be company employees, earn salaries, and receive corporate dividends that are tax-free if the distribution does not exceed their stock basis. If dividends exceed a shareholder's stock basis, the excess is taxed as capital gains—but these are taxed at a lower rate than ordinary income.

Other advantages include being able to transfer interests or adjust property basis, without facing adverse tax consequences or having to comply with complex accounting rules.

Finally, S corporation status may help establish credibility with potential customers, employees, suppliers, and investors by showing the owner's formal commitment to the company.

Disadvantages of Filing Under Subchapter S

Because S corporations can disguise salaries as corporate distributions to avoid paying payroll taxes, the IRS scrutinizes how S corporations pay their employees. An S corporation must pay reasonable salaries to shareholder-employees for services rendered before any distributions are made.

When it comes to making those distributions to stakeholders, the S Corp must allocate profits and losses based strictly on the percentage of ownership or number of shares each individual holds.

If an S Corp does not—or if it makes any other noncompliance moves, like mistakes in an election, consent, notification, stock ownership, or filing requirement—the IRS could terminate its Subchapter S status. This happens rarely, though. Usually, a quick rectification of non-compliance errors can avoid any adverse consequences.

Filing under Subchapter S also requires time and money—or more precisely, the business of setting up a corporation does. The business owner must submit articles of incorporation with the Secretary of State in the state where their company is based. The corporation must obtain a registered agent for the business, and it pays other fees associated with incorporating itself.

In many states, owners pay annual report fees, a franchise tax, and other miscellaneous fees. However, the charges are typically inexpensive and may be deducted as a cost of doing business. Also, all investors receive dividend and distribution rights, regardless of whether the investors have voting rights.

Finally, there are the qualification requirements. The limits on the number and the nature of shareholders might prove onerous for a business that is growing rapidly and wants to attract venture capital or institutional investors.

Pros

- Tax benefits: no or lesser corporate and self-employment tax for owner, no double taxation for shareholders

- Protections of incorporation: limited liability, transfer of interests

- Prestige, credibility

Cons

- Costs of incorporation

- Complex compliance rules

- Potentially growth-inhibiting qualifications to maintain status

S Corp vs. LLC

A limited liability company (LLC) is another type of legal business entity. Like the S Corp, it is a common go-to structure for small businesses.

LLCs and S corps share other characteristics as well. Both are pass-through entities, meaning they do not pay corporate taxes, and both offer limited liability protection for their owners/principals, meaning the owners' personal assets cannot be touched by business creditors, nor can they be held personally responsible in lawsuits filed against the company.

However, LLCs are more flexible than S corps. They are not subject to the IRS regulations concerning the number and type of shareholders/owners (called "members"), or to other federal or state rules regarding governance, procedure, and distribution of funds. They can allocate their profits and losses in whatever proportions the owner's desire.

Easier to establish than S corps, LLCs typically are formed by sole proprietors or small groups of professionals, like attorneys, doctors, or accountants. However, their financing options are more limited to bank loans, as opposed to equity investors. This can limit their potential for growth.

U.S. Income Tax Return for an S Corporation

Although they are exempt from corporate taxes, S corporations must still report their earnings to the federal government and file tax returns.

Form 1120-S is an S Corp's tax return. Often accompanied by a Schedule K-1, which delineates the percentage of company shares owned by each individual shareholder, Form 1120-S reports the income, losses, dividends, and other distributions the corporation has passed onto its shareholders.

Unlike C corps, which must file quarterly, S corps only file once a year, like individual taxpayers. Form 1120-S is simpler than tax forms for C corporations, too. The version for 2020 ran five pages.

If a company elects S corporation status (and the IRS has accepted that election), it must file Form 1120-S. The form is due by the 15th day of the third month after the end of its fiscal year—generally, March 15 for companies that follow a calendar year.

Like individuals, S corporations can request a six-month extension to file their tax returns. To do so, they must file Form 7004: Application for Automatic Extension of Time To File Certain Business Income Tax, Information, and Other Returns by their return's regular due date.

S Corp FAQs

Why Would You Choose an S Corporation?

S corporations can be the best of both worlds for a small business, combining the benefits of corporations with the tax advantages of partnerships.

Specifically, S corporations offer the limited liability protection of the corporate structure—meaning an owner's personal assets cannot be accessed by business creditors or legal claims against the company. But, like partnerships, they do not pay corporate taxes on any earnings and income they generate. They can also help owners avoid self-employment tax if their compensation is structured as a salary or a stock dividend.

What Does S Corporation Stand For?

An S corporation is named for Subchapter S of Chapter 1 of the Internal Revenue Code. It has elected to be taxed under this provision of the IRS code. S corps are also known as S subchapters.

How Does an S Corp Work?

In many ways, an S Corp works as any corporation does. Operating under its home state's corporation statutes, it establishes a board of directors and corporate officers, by-laws, and a management structure. It issues shares of company stock. Its owners cannot be held personally or financially liable for claims by creditors or against the company.

S corps are distinguished by the fact that they are not federally taxed on most of the earnings they generate and distribute, leaving more money to pass to shareholders (who do pay taxes on the funds, at their ordinary-income rates). The funds must be allocated strictly based on the shareholders' equity stake or their number of shares.

S corps must restrict their number of shareholders to one hundred or less, and these must all be individuals, non-profits, or trusts. These stockholders, along with the corporation itself, must be U.S.-based.

Come tax time, S corps must distribute the form Schedule K-1 to shareholders, indicating their annual profits or losses from the company, and file Form 1120-S with the IRS.

Which Is Better, an LLC or S Corp?

Whether an LLC or an S Corp is better depends on the size and nature of the business and its aspirations for growth.

An LLC tends to be preferable for sole proprietors or enterprises with just a few partners, due to its flexibility and ease of establishment If a business is larger—or aspires to be—the S Corp might work better. S corps have more financing options: Unlike LLCs, they are allowed to offer equity stakes to investors in return for capital, for example. And if their operations are complex, they would benefit from establishing the formal structures, compliance procedures, and other protocols required of corporations.

What Is the Difference Between S Corp and C Corp?

One key difference between S corps and C corps can be expressed in one word: taxes. In a nutshell, C corps pay them, and S corps do not (mostly).

C corps pay corporate taxes on their earnings, the way individuals pay income taxes. (In the U.S., corporations are taxed currently at a flat rate of 21%.) Any dividends or other profits are then distributed to shareholders with after-tax funds. S corps, by contrast, are exempt from federal tax on most earnings—there are a few exceptions on certain capital gains and passive income—so they can distribute more gains to stockholders.

In return for this tax benefit, S corps face certain IRS-mandated restrictions. They and their shareholders must be domestically based. They can have no more than one hundred shareholders, whose ranks are limited to individuals, non-profits, trusts, and estates—no institutional investors, in other words. And they can issue only one class of stock.

C corps do not have to comply with any of these restrictions. Generally (though not always) an S Corp is smaller than a C corp.

The Bottom Line

S corporations are a common type of legal entity recommended for small businesses. They carry the tax advantages of partnerships while providing the limited liability protections of corporations. Sort of a corporate-lite structure, they are easy to establish and simpler to maintain than regular C corporations.

S corps do require many of the protocols and incur many of the costs associated with regular corporations—starting with the fees and formalities associated with incorporation. They are more expensive to establish and time-consuming to maintain than limited liability companies, another popular small-business structure.

Though advantageous for fast-growing firms, they are also subject to certain restrictions on their size and shareholder by the IRS, which could eventually inhibit their expansion. The good news is, it is easy for an S Corp to change to C corporation status, should business conditions prove favorable to do so.

What Is a C Corporation?

A C corporation (or C-Corp) is a legal structure for a corporation in which the owners, or shareholders, are taxed separately from the entity. C corporations, the most prevalent of corporations, are also subject to corporate income taxation. The taxing of profits from the business is at both corporate and personal levels, creating a double taxation situation.

C-corps can be compared with S corporations and limited liability companies (LLCs), among others, which also separate a company's assets from its owners, but with different legal structures and tax treatment. A newer type of organization is the B-corporation (or benefit corporation), which is a for-profit firm but different from C-corps in purpose, accountability, and transparency, but are not different in how they are taxed.

Key Takeaways

- A C Corporation legally separates owners' or shareholders' assets and income from that of the corporation.

- C corporations limit the liability of investors and firm owners since the most that they can lose in the business's failure is the amount they have invested in it.

- C corporations are mandated to hold annual meetings and have a board of directors that is voted on by shareholders.

How C Corporations Work

Corporations pay corporate taxes on earnings before distributing remaining amounts to the shareholders in the form of dividends. Individual shareholders are then subject to personal income taxes on the dividends they receive. Although double taxation is an unfavorable outcome, the ability to reinvest profits in the company at a lower corporate tax rate is an advantage.

A C corporation is required to hold at least one meeting each year for shareholders and directors. Minutes must be maintained to display transparency in business operations. A C corporation must keep voting records of the company's directors and a list of the owner's names and ownership percentages. Further, the business must have company bylaws on the premises of the primary business location. C corporations will file annual reports, financial disclosure reports, and financial statements.

Organizing a C Corporation

The first step in forming a C corporation is to choose and register an unregistered business name. The registrant will file the articles of incorporation with the Secretary of State according to the laws of that state. C corporations offer stock to shareholders, who, upon purchase, become owners of the corporation. The issuance of stock certificates is upon the creation of the business.

All C corporations must file Form SS-4 to obtain an employer identification number (EIN). Although requirements vary across jurisdictions, C corporations are required to submit state, income, payroll, unemployment, and disability taxes. In addition to registration and tax requirements, corporations must establish a board of directors to oversee management and the operation of the entire corporation. Appointing a board of directors seeks to resolve the principal-agent dilemma, in which moral hazard and conflicts of interest arise when an agent works on behalf of a principal.

C Corporations are the most common type of corporation, versus an S Corporation or an LLC.

Benefits of a C Corporation

C corporations limit the personal liability of the directors, shareholders, employees, and officers. In this way, the legal obligations of the business cannot become a personal debt obligation of any individual associated with the company. The C corporation continues to exist as owners change and members of management are replaced.

A C corporation may have many owners and shareholders. However, it is required to register with the Securities and Exchange Commission (SEC) upon reaching specific thresholds. The ability to offer shares of stock allows the corporation to obtain substantial amounts of capital which may fund new projects and future expansions.

What is a Nonprofit Organization?

A nonprofit organization is a business that has been granted tax-exempt status by the Internal

Revenue Service (IRS) because it furthers a social cause and provides a public benefit. Donations made to a nonprofit organization are typically tax-deductible to individuals and businesses that make them, and the nonprofit itself pays no tax on the received donations or on any other money earned through fundraising activities. Nonprofit organizations are sometimes called NPOs or 501(c)(3) organizations based on the section of the tax code that permits them to operate.

Qualifications for NPO Status

A nonprofit designation and tax-exempt status are given only to organizations that further religious, scientific, charitable, educational, literary, public safety or cruelty-prevention causes or purposes. Examples of nonprofit organizations include hospitals, universities, national charities, churches, and foundations.

A nonprofit must serve the public in some way, whether through the offering of goods, services, or a combination of the two. They're also required to make financial and operating information public so that donors can be informed about how—and how well—their contributions have been used.3 Nonprofits may also exist to collect income to dispense to other qualifying charities.

Before it can receive a tax exemption, an organization needs to request 501(c)(3) status from the IRS. Once registered and running, the organization has to maintain compliance with the appropriate state agency that regulates charitable organizations. This often requires a dedicated CIO and accounting team.

NPOs cannot be political, which helps explain why so many of them actively seek a non-partisan tone in their communications. Organizations seeking 501(c)(3) status must state explicitly in their organizing papers that they will not participate in any political campaign on the behalf of any candidate or make expenditures for political purposes.4 There are 501(c) groups that can engage in these activities, but not 501(c)(3) organizations.

Operating Rules for NPO Status

While some not-for-profit organizations use only volunteer labor, many large or even medium-size non-profits are likely to require a staff of paid full-time employees, managers, and directors. Despite having special tax advantages in other respects, nonprofits typically must pay employment taxes and abide by state and federal workplace rules in the same way as for-profit organizations.

Nonprofits are allowed to provide assets or income to individuals only as fair compensation for their services. Indeed, the organization must explicitly state in its organizing papers that it will not be used for the personal gain or benefit of its founders, employees, supporters, relatives, or associates.

Nonprofit vs. Not-for-Profit

The terms nonprofit organization (NPO) and not-for-profit organization (NFPO)are sometimes used interchangeably. There are, however, key distinctions between the two types of enterprise.

A key one is their purpose. As mentioned, nonprofits must offer some social benefit and provide goods or services. Not-for-profits need not have such an orientation and may exist simply to serve their membership rather than society at large.

The sections of the IRS's 501(c) code that governs each of NPOs and NFPOs serve to further delineate their differences. Nonprofits operate under 501(c)(3), for "corporations, funds or foundations that operate for religious, charitable, scientific, literary or educational purposes." NFPOs, by contrast, primarily do so under other sections, such as 501(c)(7), for "recreational organizations." One classic example of an NFPO, then, is a sports club that's jointly owned by its members and sustained simply for their enjoyment.

In turn, the code sets out different tax treatment for NPOs and NFPOs. In general, both organization types are tax-exempt, as in the income they earn is not subject to tax. But only with NPOs is the money people give to the organization, as dues or donations, deductible from their taxable income.

What Are the Articles of Incorporation?

Articles of incorporation are a set of formal documents filed with a government body to legally document the creation of a corporation. Articles of incorporation generally contain pertinent information, such as the firm's name, street address, agent for service of process, and the amount and type of stock to be issued.

Articles of incorporation are also referred to as the "corporate charter," "articles of association," or "certificate of incorporation."

Key Takeaways

- Articles of incorporation are the pertinent filing with a government body (usually the state) that signifies the creation of a corporation.

- In the U.S., articles of incorporation are filed with the Office of the Secretary of State where the business chooses to incorporate.

- Broadly, articles of incorporation should include the company's name, type of corporate structure, and number and type of authorized shares.

- Bylaws work in conjunction with the articles of incorporation to form the legal backbone of the business.

Understanding Articles of Incorporation

Many businesses in the U.S. and Canada are formed as a corporation, which is a type of business operation that is formed in the state where the company carries out its operations. To be recognized legally as a corporation, a business must incorporate by taking certain steps and making certain decisions required under corporate law. One such step is filing a document known as articles of incorporation.

Articles of incorporation are in the document necessary to register a corporation with a state and acts as a charter to recognize the establishment of a corporation. The document outlines the basic information needed to form a corporation, the governance of a corporation, and the corporate statutes in the state where the articles of incorporation are filed.

Special Considerations

In the U.S., articles of incorporation are filed with the Office of the Secretary of State in the state where the business chooses to incorporate. Some states offer more favorable regulatory and tax environments and, as a result, attract a greater proportion of firms seeking incorporation.

For example, Delaware and Nevada attract about half of the public corporations in the U.S., in part because of the state laws that protect their corporations. Once established, the articles become a public record and provide important information about the corporation.

Requirements for Articles of Incorporation

The articles in the document vary by state, but the following "articles" are typically included:
1. Name of corporation

2. Name and address of the registered agent

3. Type of corporate structure (e.g., profit corporation, nonprofit corporation, non-stock corporation, professional corporation, etc.)

4. Names and addresses of the initial board of directors

5. Number and type of authorized shares

6. Duration of the corporation if it wasn't established to exist perpetually

7. Name, signature, and address of the incorporator, who is the person in charge of setting up a corporation
Most states also require the articles to state the firm's purpose, though the corporation may define its purpose very broadly to maintain flexibility in its operations. Amazon's certificate of incorporation, for example, states that the corporation's purpose is "to engage in any lawful act or activity for which corporations may be organized under the General Corporation Law of Delaware."

Other provisions outlined in a company's articles of incorporation may include the limitation of the directors' liability, actions by stockholders without a meeting, and the authority to call special meetings of stockholders. Each state has certain mandatory provisions that must be contained in the articles of incorporation and other optional provisions that the company can decide whether to include.

Many states charge filing fees for a business that incorporates in the state, whether the business operates there or not. A business that is incorporated in one state and is physically located or doing business in another state must register in the other state as well, which involves paying that state's filing fees and taxes.

Depending on the state of incorporation, a company may pay filing fees ranging from $50 (as in Iowa3 , Arkansas4 , and Michigan5) to $275 (as in Massachusetts) 6 as of 2020. The fees can vary depending on whether the articles of incorporation were filed online or by mail.

Another key corporate document is the bylaws, which outlines how the organization is to be run. Bylaws work in conjunction with the articles of incorporation to form the legal backbone of the business. – You can google this and get a lot of different ones for free.

Now that you have an overview as to what the different companies are – this should give you more information before starting your company. Keep working hard and see you at the bank.

CPSIA information can be obtained
at www.ICGtesting.com
Printed in the USA
LVHW070951160122
708696LV00002B/90